TO BANGLADESH WITH LOVE

SAMIT DHAR

Made with ♥ on the Notion Press Platform
www.notionpress.com

TO THE LOVELY PEOPLE OF BANGLADESH

Contents

CHAPTER ONE

TO BANGLADESH WITH LOVE

It has been years now ,recollection seems a bit foggy .I remember crossing the mighty Jamuna bridge after Bogura and moving deep into the land of my forefathers.There was probably pretty tension back home. Dad and Mom must have been tossing in bed through a sleepless night thinking of their only son who had never stayed away from them for more than a day or two, in his whole life,now in a different country hundreds of miles away from them.Dawn opened up as the bus screeched to a halt in the outskirts of Dhaka.I could see broad streets lined with closed shops.I could perhaps see my future in Bangladesh,with someone I loved.I was energetic and bubbling with excitement as I rode a rickshaw to Dhanmondi .The school gates were closed.The watchman told me to wait till 8 AM.He was stupefied that I had come such a long way to teach .He was kind to offer me tea.The administrative building was impressive and I was escorted to a waiting hall at 8 AM.It was the Skylark International school.I had taught in many schools in India but this was different, this was IGCSE ,Cambridge .The British Council trained the teachers ,helped them prepare the students and arranged for the

IGCSE examinations .I was taken to the room of Md.Malek,he was third in rank at the Skylark main section after the Principal,the first being the President.On seeing my appointment letter he told that he was glad to see me from across the border in his office ,especially a young Bengali gentleman who had come to teach in Bangladesh.He asked in excellent English about my qualifications and my background ,my university.He wanted to know about North Bengal University.He corrected me when I said that in North Bengal we have only one university,he said “WestBengal “is an undivided state of India then why did we say south and north. I stated about the geographical location of the two parts of the same state on the South and North of the Ganges made us say so ,there was nothing about any administrative , political ,social barriers .He proudly said that Bengalis on both the side of the borders be it his or mine were the same, creative and innovative.Soon I was instructed about the section and part of the school where I would begin my teaching and sent to the flat in the next street in a car along with a person named Zakir from the school office. The flat was fully furnished and I was told the necessary protocols .Zakir told me about a lady teacher also from India who was given the next flat opposite mine from the school .Soon I unpacked and thought about what Babu and Ma was doing at that time it was 9 AM ,I was just half an hour ahead in time.This half an hour early had brought me to a place where earlier my ancestors once tilled the green,fertile fields. I have to ring back home I ought to find a booth from where I can call. Soon I had my bath .There was a refrigerator ,it was stocked with bread butter ,chips, eggs.The gas oven was operational.I made an omelette and sat back on a chair.I thought of my girl was she awake

?Was she thinking of me ? I would see her again after months .It pained me but I thought of the prestige and the salary I would achieve in Dhaka .Her parents would not disagree to give her in marriage with me and settle here in Dhaka.Again I was counting my chickens before they hatched. Back in Kolkata months before, I had appeared in an interview at the Great Eastern. The President of the school and his wife the Principal of the main section had told me about many deserving candidates who were offered the job and I was one of them.

I was told to get my work permit and passport in order to join Skylark. It took me long debates and even heated exchanges with Babu and Ma that I was determined to go to Bangladesh and try my luck in a reputed school there rather than waiting, remaining jobless for some more years and seeing my love being married to someone else.Years later I now think that I had really counted my chickens before they hatched.What was I to do? I was a romantic.Why would not I be?The authors sitting in the library shelves of North Bengal University were all of the opinion that life should be experienced in as much colours as possible.

The door bell rang, I was just resting a bit and gathering myself up to teach my first IGCSE class the next day.I opened the door, a young woman introduced herself as Ankana Mitra ,from Kolkata in India.She was the English language teacher under contract service fom India just like I was ,she had arrived a few months earlier.She lived in the flat opposite to me.We talked about the unemployment problems of both the countries.She said that she also had her ancestral roots in Bangladesh.

The next day saw me the a great any challenges.The section to which I was send the full time section, was a residential area with big gardens.I was taken to the full time section

Principal 's office .She was the school physician's wife.She was very friendly.She was from India .She told me how she had met with her husband for the first time in Russia where they had both gone to study but in different streams. It was love that brought her to be married and settle in Bangladesh. In the afternoon I was told to explain a poem in class viii,then I was moved to class ix where I had to explain a bit of Macbeth.The students seemed to be impressed. I was taken to the library and given a card so that I could use the reference books there for teaching.I was told by the Principal that I was to reach school everyday at quarter to 8 in the morning so that I could check the uniform of students as they entered .If they would not wear it properly they were to be rounded off and packed to the Principal's office. Then I was greeted by the dining manager of that section who told me that he was instructed by the Main section Principal that I was to be given an additional duty of standing and supervising lunch when the students would eat .The discipline was not to be broken at any cost.I was even given another duty to inspect the kitchen twice a week for the right maintenance of cleanliness and hygiene.Phewwwww! I thought what would I be at the end of the day but they were paying me a hefty sum that was true.I met Mitra at the end of the day she said she was teaching in the same section but was to be taken over to the main because I had arrived.

Soon I was rushing in and out of the full time section of the Skylark International school.The students after lunch sat for solving their homework in which we assisted them.They would go back home at 5 and would not have to bother about the homework for next day.I soon started fitting in among the students of class VI,VII,VII,IX,X .They at first had many questions in their mind especially class

VI.One of the girls I still remember her name Sahida who used to go back with me in the school bus, oneday told me that I looked like a Bangladeshi citizen .I could not be an Indian.I chuckled and told her that we were once people of an undivided country .She was confused.I asked her again how she had that in mind. She said my way of teaching them ,cracking jokes , looking after them while they had lunch made her think that it was impossible for an Indian to mingle so much with them.I laughed and told that she was a little girl ,she had a lot to know , God made land and man made borders.I was just like the other teachers in their school who were Bangladeshis ,only I belonged to a different nation ,India. We have the same blood and flesh.Sahida and her friends one day in a free period sat with me and had many of their queries answered.How I grew up ?Where and how my parents were? They all seemed surprised that in India I grew up in the same way they were growing up. I told them that oneday my ancestors had lived in a place called Gharinda in this lush green country .It was sad that they had to depart to India after partition.Black,white and bright colours are a part of life and in our life time we all have to experience all of them.Sahida and her friends were of the opinion that may be if the British wouldn't have arrived at all in our part of the continent we would remain unified. I replied that it would have been better if it would have been so , still we can remain unified in our hearts and minds.Barbed wire borders of our countries cannot stop beautiful feelings and ideas from mingling.

The Principal of the Main section of Skylark International ,a very smart lady was the wife of the President of the Skylark International school.She was a Barracuda to teachers who were found to be casual about their duties.

She spoke English like Memsahibs.Even the guards who looked like bouncers at the school gates, never ever looked her in the eye.

Soon I was to embark on a new course of the British council that was a compulsory one for all the teachers of Skylark International school.I was really looking forward to the session with all Sahibs ,Memsahibs in their stiff collars and trousers ,blazers teaching us the latest technique of teaching . The day arrived and I was packed off in a school bus with a couple of other teachers to the massive building in an area near the British High Commission. The classes were impressive ,while others scribbled data in their note books , I looked at the Hi fi projectors and the laser indicators in the hands of the instructors. I thought that teaching the British a lesson to leave our country wasn't perhaps enough as they had returned to teach us again.It was lunch time and I was very happy to see the world famous Bangladeshi Hilsa on the buffet table .This was a thing which was drooled upon by me since my childhood .The smell of fried Hilsa, coming out from the kitchen with my mother busy over the oven and Babu reading a newspaper again and again during the rainy evenings with flooded streets outside is a cherished memory. Therefore like King Arthur I swooped upon the Hilsas with silver spears. Soon I found it difficult to separate the bones from the flesh of the Hilsa and gave up my spear and dug in with my fingers (that is a must if one wants to enjoy Hilsa at it's quintessence) standing behind a big pillar unnoticiable by the people in the dining hall.How ever one of the British instructors who was helping himself with mutton caught sight of me smiled and came over at my side of the pillar. He said that he had heard that a new Indian teacher had come ,if it was me ?I replied in the affirmative. I talked less and ate more as I had lifted four pieces of the fried Hilsa at one go from the buffet table.Anyhow ,I had to complete my Hilsa course before another course began in the lecture hall. The young instructor asked how it was possible for a man to eat so many pieces of bony fish ,in such a short time ,it was no better than running through a minefield,anytime the throat could be a victim of pain and terrible discomfort.Well, I said with a smile we Bengalis are dexterous with fishes of any water and type .I added that perhaps this patience along with the dexterity with which we deal Hilsa on our plates helped us to get through all the complex atrocities inflicted upon us by the British before independence in the then unified Bengal .After the lunch was over I still had twenty minutes in hand before the second half began. The instructor was eager to show me the facility ,especially the audio video room where the students are brought in once a month for special classes by the teachers of British Council.The instructor said that he was interested in visiting all the places worth seeing in Bangladesh. He wanted to know how similar were the Indians with the Bangladeshis. I said that once we were together but now are two nations.Two nations who co operate with each other in fields of education ,medicine, technology ,agriculture,infrastructure .Moreover a state in India named West Bengal to where I belong, is a place where we speak the same language Bengali. Ofcourse there are some variations in Bangladesh such as the Dhakaiya where the Bengali language ,pronunciations ,accents are a bit different.I told him how before independence many freedom fighters had hailed from this soil fighting the British .I told him that he had come to a country where people had laid down their lives for the recognition of their language .True,without the freedom of the mother tongue we cannot be better than slaves.The Bengalis of Bangladesh had been brave enough to fight a superior power and attain their right of mother tongue. At present, we ,both the nations Bangladesh and India are the upcoming powers in South Asia, paving our way to a better economy and one day ,we will dominate the world economy with the huge number of human and natural resources we have.The young instructor was happy to have a friend like me except for the burps I gave out after completing those big pieces of Hilsa .After the course was over, the school bus dropped me off at the school.A rickshaw took me to my flat,I took a bath and went to sleep.Late in the evening I had to make a small meal for myself as I was still heavy with the six pieces of steamed ,mustard Hilsa I had at the training session.The refrigerator was half stocked with eggs ,some vegetables which I had bought from the local market.I decided to make an omellete for dinner but realised that I had no cooking oil left in the kitchen. I thought of going to the next flat to Mitra and see if she could give me some. I rang the bell a maid opened the door ,she was the cooking maid which Mitra had kept for herself .I told my plight .Soon I was siting in the drawing room of Mitra's flat and sipping tea. We talked about our university courses .Her being Calcutta University and my being North Bengal University.We both were of the same opinion about the warm reception we received in a new nation .I told about the Custom officials who were very friendly and appreciated my coming in to their country to teach. The senior officers had ordered their subordinates to do my immigration work as fast as possible.The border guards too were happy to see an Indian venture into their country to teach. Even the officials at Bangladesh High commission were glad about my choice of teaching in Bangladesh and happily chatted with me about their land and me going to the land where my ancestors once lived before the partition took place.

Mitra had her home in the suburbs of Kolkata .She had come to Bangladesh a few months before me. She had become a close friend of the Principal of the main section.

I went back to my flat I had my omlette and I laid down thinking of someone who meant a lot to me other than my parents. I remember the day on which I was on my way to Kolkata , to get my work permit when Babu askcd why just for a girl I was so bent upon getting a job in Bangladesh ,there were jobs too in India .He asked why I was going back to a land from where my ancestors had to come away.I told him that she was just not a girl ,she was a special one,she meant a lot to me for whom I needed a prestigious job so that I could be able to put forward a proposal to her father about giving her hand in marriage with me in a few years. Babu told me if I was sure that she would marry me. I replied in the positive. I wished I had a mobile with an international SIM so that I could talk to Babu ,Ma and her.I saw that Mitra had one . I thought of getting one soon.

The week began with Sunday and I found myself standing near the gate of the full time section for an hour before the school began with the national anthem .There were female and male teachers both in the full time section. I remember one Mrs.Khan who was very loving and kind lady who often invited me to come at her house but i never got the time since I would be busy after 5 exploring Dhaka .After 8 PM I had also to cook my dinner at my flat since I had not been lucky enough like Mitra to get a cook .

I was eager on Fridays to talk to my girl across the border .The international calls were costly .So we decided to fix a time on Friday evening when she would be in a cyber café and I too .We would chat for one hour once a week and I used to ring her at her home on Sunday evenings.I knew her father did not approve of me much but he didn't object either.Moreover my girl's mom was on my side.I remember that I used to spend less time thinking about Babu and Ma and think more of her.I would think how after a couple of years I would be able to marry her and bring her to Dhaka ,what type of flat we would rent or stay in the same one given by my school.The days passed to months and soon it was the time when I could visit Siliguri, after the Durga Puja was over. I came to Siliguri and went straight to her home from the airport .I now regret how Babu and Ma waited for me on the 1st floor veranda to see me and I was busy at my girl's place.Was it because of her magical attraction ?Her love that I had been so transformed? My girl was happy to see me and so were her parents. It seemed paradise was near .The way my Girl and her parents behaved ,marriage was a near call only after she would finish her Masters in North Bengal University .It was a short stay and I spent most of the day time with my girl on my bike ,shooting like a meteor through the green jungles of Doars and having moments steeped in romance at restaurants.I remember one day she was to come to my house .On the last day of my stay in Siliguri it was agreed that she would come to my house at about 4 in the evening. She was late .I was getting impatient .A call came on my landline .My girl told me not to venture out of my house ,she would come soon .She said she would come within half an hour. She arrived after 2 hours. I asked her why she was late especially on the last day of my stay .The next day I would leave for the border at Burimari.I jokingly said she must be having a new boyfriend as I was away for months.I thought she either would laugh or be angry at me.To my utter surprise she suddenly stooped down and caught my feet and said to forgive her.I asked what should I forgive her for?She was silent .After a minute she said that she meant that she was sorry for being late.I said, I respected, her trusted her fully and it was awkward for me to have her touch my feet. Soon I was moving across the Bangladeshi soil .Babu and Ma probably felt sad with their son who spent most of the time of his brief stay with his girl. After crossing Bogura my bus stopped before crossing the Jamuna bridge at a motel . People were busy eating .I took a plate of rice and Chitol .The Chitol was really like butter as it was a fresh catch form Jamuna. The next dawn, I was on a rickshaw towards Dhanmondi where my flat was. My heart was a bit heavy, I knew I would not be home before six months.

Mitra was not back at her flat and school was to begin after two days. I had to attend to training programmes at the school hall.With free time in the afternoon I decided to go and meet Shishir , a teacher who was a devoted follower of Loknath Baba. His son was a student in class VII at the full time section .He told about the academic and career development of students in Bangladesh .Students went in large numbers to Australia and European countries as they excelled in their studies. With scholarships from the Bangladeshi government, bright students in Bangladesh had enough prospects to develop even if they were from rural , poor background.I decided to go to Barodi with a colleague of mine ,Shisir .Barodi ,the holy place of Loknath Baba and the ancestral home of the famous, late Ex - Chief minister of WestBengal ,Jyoti Basu. At the Loknath mandir there, probably ,I found strength to withstand the grilling that would unexpectedly come on my way ahead.

In Siliguri, where I grew up and studied at Mahbert High school I heard my teachers say that a man reaps as he sows.

I had sowed well but did not get a good harvest atleast as far as Cupid is concerned.My girl who was to chat with me atleast once a week sitting in a cyber café remained absent and gave excuses like truant students whom I taught in my classes at the Skylark International.When I rang her up, she seemed very sweet and with every excuse she gave, I melted again and again.I had a firm belief that we were made for each other. Things began to roll rapidly.She was to study master's in the nearby university but chose far away New Delhi,JNU as her destination.I talked to her .She said it was a better opportunity. I agreed. Soon she was away in New Delhi. With almost 2000kms difference perhaps the relation had come to the tearing point of the stretchability of a chewing gum which only I seemed to be chewing.Soon she replied haughtily over mails and chatting was a far call. She had a mobile but when I rang in the evenings she hardly picked up.Oneday she picked up and said I should not ring her so often as she remains in the library in the evenings . When I mentioned about coming to Siliguri during holidays she replied that she had no plans in the near future ,New Delhi was a place of fast life and go- getters,she was no longer an average girl now ,she planned to climb the ladder of her career fast.I said that I had no objecton to that but atleast we should communicate once a week via Yahoo messenger chatting or talking for a couple of minutes over phone.She replied in the negative and added that I should change myself as she had changed.That was a reply which made my loveline go bleak .I could neither speak to her nor get any replies to my mails .I rang Babu Ma routinely but my heart had gone dry.My voice caught on a different tone and Babu once asked me if something was wrong. I replied in the negative. What was I going to tell them ?The girl for whom I had taken up a job so far away, was no longer interested in me? I had often cooked up a storm at home when Ma objected to my love for her and my decision to go to Bangladesh just to prove my ability that I was good enough for her.I had crossed borders to remain united but borders had come up in my private world.These borders were with fences where no passport and visas could help me.The fences of the mind and heart .

Compressing my feelings and eating them down like a KFC burger was the only solution at that time as I was alone and neither could I talk to anyone about this in Dhaka nor had I the face to tell Babu and Ma about it.At the Skylark International I tried my best to keep my personal feelings away from my profession,teaching the students who came from the higher rungs of the society.They were lovely with inquisitive minds and a very sweet approach to an Indian who had come from across the border just to teach them.I remember one boy in standard viii who was nick named Akram Mobile by his class mates.His only habit was to change his position from one desk to the other at any moment when the teacher was looking down at the text or writing on the white board.This jolly young fellow had become one of my favourite students during my stay at Skylark International.Days rolled on .I was getting attached to the life in Dhaka.Only somewhere within, a fire burnt ,the smoke of which could not be seen but smelt.

During lunch hours it was my duty to stand in the dining hall of the school to observe the students and to see that they ate in a disciplined way.I was given lunch too after the lunch hour for the students ended and I gulped it down during off periods. The school was totally different from the ones I had worked in India. The yearly increment depended upon the performance of the teacher. The Principal of the main section had long queues of teachers in front of her office waiting for their name to be announced for the increment interview . Teachers who performed well were given increment and others went home with a sad face of a child denied it's much desired lollipop. The principal was a straight forward lady and her talk was sharp.On my turn at the end of the year as I was ushered into her office I found myself with a dry throat sitting in front of a Barracuda with glasses. She saw through my performance card prepared by the Quality control cell and told that I would get an increment but added that the reference books in the showcase in my flat was provided by the school so that I could encrich myself to teach the students but I was not using them on holidays instead I had made myself busy going for movies and visiting malls. I fell from the sky without a parachute , How on Earth! She had someone watching over me .Was anyone from the other overseas teachers who lived in the same apartment to whom I talked freely about the movies I went on holidays , informing her? I decided that I should be moving somewhere else where she would not be able to use a drone to keep a watch on my weekly entertainments.The next month I applied to have the rent of my lodgings to be added with my salary so that I could stay in a rented flat in another locality .

When my girls birthday was near I bought a set of beautiful metal bangles from Gausia market and parceled it off to New Delhi. I rang her she did not pick up. Mails were the unanswered too. I rang her mom after a month. She said that my girl had received the bangles she had appreciated them but had sent them to her parents in Siliguri because someone might steal them at her hostel. With a break of a few days during the Durga Puja I went back to Siliguri. As I crossed over to the Indian side a senior customs official told me that it was a matter of great surprise that I had gone for employment in Bangladesh and not found one in my own country,which was vast. I smiled and told him that the whole planet is a Man's vast country .What does it matter in which corner of the same he was teaching in?He looked at me in a confused manner.

It was my Birthday, Ma had made preparations to make Payesh at home but I was mentally in New Delhi. Just on the evening before my birthday I rang at my girls mobile.After several unanswered calls ,she picked up to my great joy.I told her if she would not wish me at 12 midnight just as she did before. She said that there was not enough balance left in her phone so she wished me then and there. At night I rang her again the calls were unanswered,then it was switched off. My battery was drained . The screen of my brain flickered and tried hard to stay on. I told myself perhaps I was getting too busy with my birthday and should not have disturbed her at midnight.

The next days in Siliguri were bumpy as I went into my girls house to meet her parents .They told me that they had bright plans for their daughter as she was in a premium University now she would certainly be rocket-propelled to be a lecturer.They further added that they would not get their daughter married with some teacher in any private school in India or abroad and I should either be a government school teacher in India or be a lecturer in a government college as it was a matter of status for them. When I asked them whether their daughter was also of the same opinion?They replied in the positive.I rang her directly from there and she said that she was of the same opinion of her parents and it was for the greater good.She added that I was thinking and planning future illogically.

After coming out of their house I felt myself like a floating plankton.

In Siliguri I still had a few more days in hand. What would I do?Most of my friends were busy in their own offices, some were gone to other places . I had my bike .I took a long ride through the forests but it did not suffice. I told Babu to come with me oneday and he was more than pleased. I went to a jewellery shop and bought Ma a diamond ring . To my surprise her face did not glow as I expected she said that she was happy to have such a gift but she wished me to return . They went over the same epic of having only one son away from them during their old age and feeling lonely. This word 'lonely' was significant one and perhaps at that time nobody understood it better than I did. I felt for Babu and Ma ,I asked myself repeatedly if in the pursuit of a mirage I had neglected Babu and Ma.Even if it would turn out to be a mirage , I could not just leave my job in Bangladesh and return like a coward. Wordsworth ,Byron ,Shelley, Shakespeare, Keats and my teachers Mrs.Sanyal,Mr. Mathews, Mrs Bansal,Mrs Chakraborty,Mrs .Roy, Mr Mullick , Mrs. Gitali Choudhury,Mr .Mukherjee, Mrs. Phillips ,Mr. Nelson Petrie, Mrs. Winnie Petrie, Mr. Ajay Choudhary, Mr. Dipak Choudhury, Mr.Katham, Mr. Ansari,Mrs. Arundhati did not teach me escapism while I studied at Mahbert High School. Moreover, I had a lovely group of students who loved and respected me a lot . I remember some of my students had wanted photographs of the jungles,hills of Terai,which I told, I frequented on my bike during my university days. I went on a ride took the shots to be taken to Dhaka. My new landlord Mr. Ruhul Amin that is of my new rented flat where I had shifted to had wanted a good pressure cooker. With all these packed I set off once again to my work field trying to avoid seeing the tearful eyes of my parents. In the bus to Dhaka I stared at the huge studded night sky and felt like a dry leaf moving with the wind.

The dawn saw me with smiling Dhaka asking me the reason of my grim face. That day I walked into the class VIII section A and explained a drama of Shakespeare.Joyraj Paul a student in my class told me that he would love to have tutions from me on Fridays .I declined . I learnt from him how he wanted to be a cricketer and how he was already being promoted by the Bangladesh Government both financially and logistically to bring out his talent in the field.This bright eyed boy wanted to play for his country . I learnt from him how his elder brother had gone to Australia to study Chemistry and was now sending home dollars to support his family. I asked about whether he would love to go to India and work there instead of following his brother . He said he had only one aim that is to play for his country. As an Indian working in Bangladesh I had to enlist my name or to inform the Indian Embassy that I was here in Dhaka .For some small formalites I went there and I was greeted by one Mr. Singh who was from New Delhi. He missed it very much. He told me that in case of any difficulty I could come to him at the office.

The Skylark school administration held a small party at a five star hotel where the President ,the Vice President and the Main Section Head co ordinators were present. There I met a man who was dressed in black suit ,black tie he was about 60yrs old .When he heard that I was from India he told me that when he was young like me he had fought for Bangladesh . He told me how Indian airforce used it's transport planes to evacuate the Bangladeshi freedom fighters .How in high altitude his fellow soldiers became sick and how on arriving at Bagdogra airforce station they were given refreshing lemon tea,the taste of which lingers in his memories.Some sad ,painful memories also lingers in his mind such as the martyrd freedom fighters who fell while fighting,how they buried them and how they had to chase away jackals who dug up the graves to eat the flesh at night.He said that young men like me who ever it be whether from Bangladesh or India made him feel that there is much that we can achieve together.He explained how Bangladesh was now a place which had immense prospects in textiles,agriculture,fisheries.He added that we two neighbouring countries had only one common enemy that is poverty and we should strive hard together to erase it. I was requested by the President of my school to deliver a speech on the contribution of Bengalis in modern world economy . I stumbled with veterans and my senior administrative officials sitting around.

Dhaka was beautiful ,especially when I saw it with the stormy nimbus clouds churning up a storm over the Buriganga . My new rented flat at Mohammadpur had three floors.It belonged to one of the music teachers of our section.Her father Mr.Ruhul Amin was a retired Electric engineer.He was a kind man who called me Babu exactly like my own father called me at home. The top floor where I stayed had tiled roof .During storms at night I had to move into the toilet as it had a concrete roof . I stayed there as long as the storm raged on.I had selected this instead of the posh flat of my school to be free on Fridays without being pryed upon by other overseas teachers and it worked.Mitra had warned me that it would not be safe for an Indian teacher ,a newcomer but I found that it was nothing of the kind be it in Dhaka or elsewhere in Bangladesh. My short trips to Chittagong, the long natural sea beaches of Cox Bazar,the Aggameda Khyang monastery with centuries old manuscripts ,bronze statues,the tropical rainforest of

Himchari National park were wonderful indeed.Bangladesh was a country where I received warm acceptance wherever I went.At my new lodgings in Dhaka I was ok except for the storms at night.

As months rolled on with busy schedules of training and teaching and preparing the kids for their exams. I was not able to speak over the phone or chat via Yahoo messenger with my girl.She had mentioned in one of her mails not to disturb her as she was preparing for her exams and she wanted to be in the creamy layer.After a long spell of keeping mum I wrote a long letter to her about how we rode down the winding path of the hills of Kurseong ,Darjeeling,Doars and how I wished that we would move in the same way together on the winding path of life. In reply my girl sent me a nuclear warhead to detonate in my mind and heart.In her mail she wrote that she found my letter very boring and my writings proved that I was nothing but a coward.She added that she had an awful headache after going through my long letter and was no longer interested in keeping any sort of relation with me.Nothing could be worse for me .This made me roam the entire Dhaka city after school hours, looking for something to cool my radioactive mind.In the evening I gave up the school cab to return to my flat . Walking over the small bridges,around the lake at Dhanmondi,taking a bus to Gulshan ,having coffee at a small joint there sitting for hours ,reading paper backs , finishing a couple of cigarettes brought me nano inches of relief.I was no longer interested in movies and malls .The mouthwatering rolls at Rifles Square were no longer tasty.In class, I appeared to the students to be a drifter usually in the second half of the day. Saidul a senior boy of class X asked me about my changes.I avoided.Soon some of the teachers over there Mr. Shishir ,Mr.

Prashant,Md.Hafizul also detected it. Oneday as I was walking back from my school across the beautiful lake near Dhanmondi these three gentlemen accompanied me to my place on the excuse that they would have a cup of tea at my place.

I found them to be the supply line to my gradually depleting energy and enthusiasm stock after the cross country nuclear attack from my girl . Hafizul narrated how a man should stand up after being struck down especially in matters of the heart Prashanta narrated his own personal experience with his beloved years ago.Shisir who was a follower of Baba Loknath told me to prepare to go to Barodi again on the next holiday for peace and calmness.Hafizul went and bought pizzas and colas ,Shisir and Prashanta sang some good Nazrul Geeti and Rabindra Sangeet .Late evening we went out for dinner at a lake side restaurant in Dhanmondi.When I returned home I found that the trio had ignited a fraction of my cold spirit ,it was enough to help me stand up and keep burning instead of being sucked up by a black hole which came close every day.

However another front opened up . Mitra was given the duty of the quality control cell of English at the full time section.After the mid session semester was over ,I had checked the scripts and sent it back to school.On one fine day I was called up by the full time section Principal .As I sat in her office she told me that I had not checked the answer scripts properly.I was shown two copies among the forty I had checked and there were about four circles with red both the scripts combined.They were some spelling mistakes .The head of quality control cell English,full time section Mitra was called in and she told me bluntly that she had made those red circles ,it was a blunder, I should not have overlooked those four spelling mistakes.I told that I had not circled some wrong spellings .Well it was not right on my part but it did not need a full barrage of artillery fire to get me corrected.She said that being a responsible teacher I should not have disgraced myself like that. I was not prepared for this skirmish. I did not say anything more.I thought how on earth did Mitra have a grudge on me ? I had not played anything foul on her except for refusing to go to the embassy together on one occasion when she had comc with a school car to pick me up from school with the permission from the main section Principal.Was it for leaving the apartment where she lived?

The school fest was on and I was with a brand new tie roaming amidst the stalls arranged in the main section playground .Mitra appeared suddenly and pulled me by the tie and said that she would put the knot properly .Before I could say anything she opened my tie , did what she had to do and put it on my neck again. Well I was not angry on her for the quality control cell matter neither was I pleased.She took me by the hand to a sweet stall ,bought a huge rosogolla and tried to thrust it into my mouth. I did not like sweets but I hardly had anytime to say no. I saw the Main section Principal the Barracuda(wife of the President of Skylark international) she was in a pleasant mood and seemed very friendly especially with Mitra. Mitra told her if she knew about my new lodgings. The smiling Barracuda asked me why I had left the apartment provided by the school and moved off on my own?I said that I was completely at peace where I had moved off. The day went on with the school fest being visited by dignitaries from the British Council.Mitra seemed to be clinging to me althrough.Perhaps she was trying to patch up the quality control cell matter but I had forgotten it already.She deliberately arranged my plate from the lunch buffet and sat next to me telling about her family in Kolkata.She told me to shift back to the school flat as it would be better for both of us to discuss the school debate competitions ,question papers etc .I declined.

My Landlord had worked in Kaptai hydroelectric project somewhere in Southeastern Bangladesh.He used to get busy telling me the various experiences he had while staying there in the quarters amidst dense jungles.He was a religious man who offered his prayers morning and evening and often told me that whatever religion one belongs to one should practice it with truth.He said all humanbeings have the same red blood running in their veins but they worship the Universal Power in different ways.His wife used to call me down to their floor when the whole family sat for lunch on fridays with any special item she made.I seemed to be a part of their family .I still remember the fine white rice rotis she made and chicken.The engineer was a master in repairing any electronic device.One winter night my room heater was not working ,it was a bitterly cold night .I had gone to watch T.V to my landlord's floor and casually mentioned about the heater.The old man offered to repair it ,I stated that I would get it repaired next day.The old man said I was too busy at school to get it repaired.The engineer soon sat with his tool box and repaired it within two hours.I felt for the old man just the same way I felt about my father at home when he pulled over the quilt on me on cold winter evenings as I fell asleep.So many years have passed by yet I long to see the engineer and his wife.Time never comes back but beautiful experiences and feelings are like incense sticks,their scent remains for long even after they are burned out fully.On one evening in the rainy seasons I had a terrible fever.Like everyday I did not go down to the landlord's floor to watch tv in the evenings ,around eight .The old man came up, saw my condition and asked if I had any medicines.I told that I had bought paracetamols while returning from school ,had them two hours ago but it seemed blunt.He went down ,came up again ,he was ready to take me to a doctor .I said it was drizzling outside and I did not want him to get wet and fall sick,he did not listen.He said that if the fever would increase at night it would be risky for me.He said that his son lived far away in Australia,he could only talk with him once a month over video calls but I would talk to him almost everyday in the evenings sitting by his side and I was no less than his son .Soon, we were on our way through the alleys of Mohammadpur on a rickshaw.The love and care of Mr.Ruhul Amin and his wife never let me feel that I was in a foreign country, far away from my parents.That night after the strong antibiotics, the fever did not have any advantage over me.

Six months had passed, I never heard again from my girl ,I managed to get up and move inspite of the cross border nuclear strike.The school was offering me a good salary,increments shoved into my pockets.At a point of time I thought of responding to Babu's proposal of returning to India and trying for a new job there.However, I thought of remaining .I was getting to learn so many new ways of modern teaching.I had so many bright students.I was meeting so many good people.Dhaka was becoming like my native town, Siliguri with so many well wishers around me.Akram who was one of my favourite students fell ill seriously and could not attend school for a week.I decided to call up his home ,I heard the tensed tone of his father that his son had been shifted to nursing home and the attending doctor had told them to immediately arrange for two units A+ blood .I had the same.When I told about this to Hafizul he said he also was with A+.So we went straight to the nursing home.After two hours Akram's family was all around me and Hafizul thanking us.Akram's father drove us back.Hafizul got down at Elephant street and I was dropped at my flat.

Oneday while as I was sitting with the students in the library during a
free period ,the President of the school came up and called me to the
Principal's chamber .I was tensed as to which quality control scan I would go under.The President was a rich man but simple.He was a man who had immense entrepreneur skills, down to earth and a Bengali to the core.When he met me in the interview for the job at The Great Eastern In Kolkata,his wife asked me
about my job experience ,the President stopped her abruptly and told me that after going through my papers he thought that I should get my visa and work permit as soon as possible and join as a Teacher at Skylark International in Dhaka .I would get everything that youngsters like me wanted starting from Pizzas to international brands of perfumes,shoes,apparels and under wear like Calvein Klein.This conversation angered his wife ,she got up and left the room.I was in a awkward situation.I thought that I would never get the appointment .I was wrong.

The President was sitted beside the Principal of the full time section .He looked serious,looking at his mobile .Was there any complain against me? I thought I better not speak ,"do not trouble ,trouble unless trouble troubles you"(One of my teachers at Mahbert High School ,Mr.Ajay Chowdhury had said) .To my relief he began with his narration about his native village at Bogura .He had set up a school there and was it's main financer.He wanted me to go to his village and teach there for couple of weeks.It was a welcome break for me but there was a glitch.The President told me that I would have to take permission from his wife the Principal of the main section as she was the head of the academics and day to day administration.

The Principal(Main Section,wife of the President of Skylark Interational) looked sternly into my eyes and said that she was not much willing to leave me for the classes in a village school because I was getting a hefty payment every month and those days when I would be away would be a loss for the school.She added that I was not going for entertainment.She added that I should hand her a written report of what I taught at Deoli the President's native village on my return to Skylark.I tried to look innocent just blinking my eyes and subdued my excitement of a welcome break in the countryside.The moment I came outside I told the attendant sitted at the door that the Barracuda almost got a piece of me.He did not understand and just bared his teeth at me.Well, I was not aware that the Barracuda had also just walked out of the office to see if her car had arrived.She heard it and I was told to report to her office the same day after the school would be over.I had butterflies in my stomach at lunch and could not eat.I was sure that my comment would get me kicked out of my job.When I was ready to leave from school the Principal of the full time section came and told me that the attendant of the Principal, main section had a message that I was to reach the Principal's house at 8 PM.I could not get a hang of the situation.Was I to get the discharge letter at her residence? I was tensed,I thought of going to the electronics shops at Baitul Mokarram ,Hafizul had once told me to visit the electronic market over there,it would amaze me.I wanted to see if amazement could suppress my fears .I roamed the shops saw the varieties of refrigerators,televisions,sound systems .I could not reduce my tension.I thought ,soon I would be hanging like a salmon before the Barracuda.I saw people in large numbers getting ready for the evening prayer .I remembered what the late President of India A.P.J Abdul Kalam had said in his Wings of Fire. He mentioned that his father Jainulabiddin Marakayar had told him that praying makes possible a communion of the spirit between people ,while praying we transcend our body and become a part of the cosmos where one cannot find any difference of anything .Probably this makes a man feel balanced even after tremendous pressure.Truly the divine power resides in all places and when one feels the thorn of losing something attached deeply , the divine power makes it up for him in a subtle way.I came to Bangladesh joyfully but after the skirmish of the New Delhi matter, I really felt tied down heavily but 'He' made it up for me by bringing to me my friends Shishir,Prashanta,Hafizul,my lovelystudents.My landlord Mr.Ruhul Amin and his wife were no less than my parents in India.In the people who were all getting ready for evening prayer there was the energy ,the joy ,the peace, the vibes of which I could feel.Unknowingly my tensions reduced.Positive energy resides in all places of prayer irrespective of religion.

When I reached the President's house he was sitted in a big green armchair ,he looked like a King about to punish a naughty countryman of his Kingdom.His wife the Principal was sitted on a Ottoman .I was told to sit .Both of them started discussing about some new car they were planning to buy.A maid servant offered tea on the small table before me.The cup remained there my throat was dry and I was in need of water but I dared not say anything.When their discussion was over the Principal told me that I was granted permission to go to the village but I should fulfill all the conditions she had put down.I swayed my head like a nursery child before a strict teacher.The President was amused at this and told his wife that she should not trouble such an innocent boy like me.In response the Principal told him with a smile that he should have heard my comment in the morning.The President asked me about it. I swallowed,stammered the Principal told that it was about some teacher which I was never to repeat in future.I tried to look innocent .The Principal told me to have the tea.I took it, swallowed the tea in one long gulp ,it was already cold with the airconditioner running in the room.

That night I was served delicious Bengali food by the Principal herself.The President proudly declared how most of the dishes were cooked by his wife ,the Principal.I could not figure out how such modern ,educated ,smart, sharp ,busy lady managing such a huge school could cook such tasty dishes.She was an ideal Bengali lady .The President talked as he ate by my side ,he told me how these dishes were made from fresh vegetables,fresh fishes.I was amazed that inspite of being one of the richest entrepreneurs in Dhaka he was so humble.That night the black Mercedes of the President dropped me at my flat at Muhammadpur.A Mercedes!!!!!! Uuuuuooowwww!!!!!I had the ride of a life time.

The next two weeks went by like a whirl wind. I took several classes at Deoli.The students were very much interested ,eager to learn.I found out that the villagers were identical to that of West Bengal,India.The elders of the village were glad to see me.They wanted to know about my parents ,my country .The President's huge village home had so many ponds with big Rohu,Chittol,Pangas and what not .I was given fresh fish fry ,fish curry, in breakfast,lunch,dinner.The President laughed when I ate ,he told that if I wished I could remain in his village home and run the school,I would be given fishes of any kind I liked, everyday.All was well except during sun downs when I roamed in the green rice fields ,I thought of my girl , my heart pained as I looked at the setting Sun in the West and thought that she must be very busy then in her class or the library with me being a forgotten past. It proved true when I went to check my mails at a cyber café at Bogura.One of my friends ,Joydeep from Siliguri had sent me photographs which were taken by me and supposed to be only with my girl.How on earth did he get it?Joydeep mentioned that these were sent to him by one of his friend who was studying law in JNU. He had sent Joydeep those photos in a mail where he proudly stated how much trust existed between himself and his girl.He(the law student) had mentioned that 'his girl' had given these all to him confessing that these were past garbage and had told him to throw them away. My friend Joydeep stated that the moment I had left for Dhaka to join my job, my girl had started a relation with this boy and both of them had planned to study in JNU together. All these Joydeep had come to know when he saw the photographs of me and my so called 'my girl'along with a brief history of lovetime written by my rival(who was already a victor, the law student) in the mail.Well, my girl was no longer my girl now and would never be, I was convinced .Now I knew why she was late on that day and had caught my feet.If she would have told me,I would have left silently.One cannot forcibly control another's feelings.I sent all these to Hafizul, Prashanta ,.Shishir in Dhaka who had become my bosom friends.Hafizul mailed back to me that he had earlier mentioned that I should get over with this chapter therefore my repetition of Paradise Lost was futile.He added that I should prepare for the IELTS with him. Shisir and Prasanta both were of the opinion that whatever had happened was not good but I should be a Man and should rejuvenate myself and look ahead .

On my return from Deoli I was kindly given a day off to prepare a concise report on my classes there.The report was enough to satisfy the main section Principal.The improvements of the students at Deoli after two weeks of classes received commendation from the teachers there.Now it was my turn to attend classes with Hafizul at a training institute in Elephant road ,Dhaka for IELTS .Hafizul had persuaded me to attend as he thought it would be of great use to me in future .I attended about three classes but soon I was seen buzzing in and around the shops at Elephant road than the coaching centre.

At the school Teachers and Guardians meet, I met many parents who were eager to talk to me as their wards had mentioned about me at home.Among them was Akram mobile's father.He had only one request that is to teach his son to be a real Man.Akram's father wanted Akram to realise the importance of honest labour before managing the family business.

At the IELTS after the other rounds were over ,I sat in the interview room with a middle aged smart British lady ,going through my performance.She asked about the films I loved to see .It was a simple answer, the films of my all time favourite the Oscar winner Mr.Satyajit Ray.She asked me the reason,I said the central theme of his films contain a universal core which has a timeless appeal .Satayajit Ray had an intellect to see through the social realities which would forever be there with man in all ages.

That day after exiting the British Council I and Hafizul

went to a good restaurant near Dhanmondi lake ,called up Prashanta,Shishir .We all sat for a couple of hours ,discussing what I would do in the near future.It was proposed that I could try for Newzealand,Australia or Britain for a career there.Hafizul would also do the same.Shisir,Prashanta would not be able to go abroad as they were married ,had children and had settled well in life, in Dhaka.I could not help digging up again the disturbing issue of my love life,I stated that it was still like a thorn in my heart.Hafizul very aptly stated that it is upon me whether the glass was half empty or half full.He said that one should have the tenacity of acceptance .I must always search for positivity instead of concentrating on the vices and putting the blame on someone.When I was with 'her' I had pure, beautiful feelings,experiences .The end was bitter but the entire experience was not.In my long bike rides with 'her ' through the forests and hills of Terai, I went through a purification process, as true love in someone never pollutes but heightens ,enhances one's soul.Hafizul said that I should be thankful to her, for bringing those heavenly moments in my life, even if it was for a short time.I agreed.

That night when I came back home, it was disturbed,I found Mr.Amin my landlord was not well he was breathing heavily.His wife was looking helpless. .A doctor had to be called.I rushed to the doctor at Mohammadpur bazar.The doctor was about to leave.He seemed annoyed to attend a house call after a long day of work.I insisted .He took his car and followed my rickshaw.It was after an injection that Mr.Amin was again breathing easily.I was relieved.His daughter our music teacher was away at a function.She came home and thanked me. I needed no thanks for doing a small service to a man who was like my father. Peace returned in my home at Dhaka.In the next week I came back from school and took my landlord for daily, short walks as the doctor had prescribed.We talked a lot about spirituality,religion and the world which is being torn apart by greed.I rang up home in Siliguri and found that my parents were planning to go to Puri for a offering a puja at Sri Jagannath temple for my safe return to a job somewhere in India.When I spoke about the IELTS and my plans to go to another country,Babu said he wanted me to return to India so that both of them would not be alone at home in their old age .I thought about my plans ,I could not say anything more.Mr.Ruhul Amin told me that I should obey my parents .He said that every Friday he prayed to Allah that his son would do well in his career but wanted him to return to Bangladesh and be by his side during his remaining days.He said the dollars that his son sent back were of no use to him .His days of material desires were over.He told me that money,career was important to me but should not be in any case, more than my parents.My Babu on the other side of the border was desiring the same.Well,now the ball was in my court but I did not know how to hit it and in which direction.

The IELTS results were out and I scored 7.5 ,Hafizul scored the same .

We partied at Shisir's house with different items of Hilsa straight from
Padma. Hafizul was preparing for going to Newzealand or Britain
wherever he would get good oppurtunities .Prashanta asked me what I
would do.I said I was a bit confused.Listening all about my confusion
Prashanta,Hafizul,Shisir told that it was my life and I was

the only one
who could take the final and best decision.
At the Skylark I was given a big responsibility for preparing forty students for the annual test.I gave my best and except a few most of them did well.Babu and Ma had come back from Puri.One evening Babu rang me up over my landlord's landline and said that he had applied on my behalf to various schools all over India ,looking up at the various advertisements in the paper and one school in Purnea in the state of Bihar had responded with an offer of a good annual package.I said I needed some time to decide.Bangladesh was a place where I learned a lot,a place where I climbed up the ladder of my career and most important of all I climbed up spiritually,a place which helped me pass through dire times ,it was not easy to leave
.

It was time for my contract to be renewed with Skylark and the necessary things were to be done regarding my work permit and multiple visa.The students had done well in their tests .Akram had scored 83 percent I was happy .One evening as I was sitting in my landlord's flat watching tv a phone call came from Babu .He said that the school administration at Purnea was more than eager to appoint me and the Vice principal of Bijay Public School ,Miss Reshma Garg had told Babu over the phone with a request that I may give her a call .I took the number down .The next day I made a call.The Vice Principal offered me the post of Academic Co ordinator along with a personal cottage within the campus for my lodging,where I could stay along with my parents.The salary offered was good too.I was told to appear for a face to face interview with the Managing Committee at my convenient date within the next month.I rang up Babu ,told the details ,he told me to take the offer.That day I had a meeting with my friends .They told that if I took the offer then my IELTS marks would not be of any use but it was a good offer if I wanted to go back to India and settle .

I told about this to my students , they all came to my table and surrounded me ,they were sure that I would turn down the offer.At the second half of the day some of them came to the dining hall while I was having lunch ,they told me that I should stay in Bangladesh and settle there.My eyes became red and moist as I felt how much they felt for me.I had lost one kind of love and won another ,far better.The summer vacation was to begin and I was to decide whether to stay or leave.After the summer vacations started I went to the President and his wife the Principal of the main section .They both told me to take the offer in Purnea and stay by my parents .Therefore I did not renew my contract.It was a pity that I could only meet a handful of the students, at their residence and could not reach all as the vacation was running.I had a talk over the phone with with Miss Reshma Garg at Purnea,all was arranged.On the day before my departure from Dhaka I had a dinner with my friends Hafizul,Shishir,Prashanta.We did not speak much except that we would always keep in touch,wherever we went.I still exchange mails with them.My landlord's wife bade me farewell with tearful eyes.My landlord,my three friends and some students came to Gabtoli to see me off. I boarded a bus which would take me to Changrabanda,Burimari border.

I miss Bangladesh which gave me so much of love and enriched my life.

9 798888 830499

Printed by Libri Plureos GmbH in Hamburg, Germany